Creative Streams

A Poet's Musings

Mitzie Holstein

Contents

Suite 300 – 852 Fort Street
Victoria, BC, Canada V8W 1H8
www.friesenpress.com

Copyright © 2014 by Mitzie Holstein
First Edition — 2014

ISBN
978-1-4602-5507-0 (Hardcover)
978-1-4602-5508-7 (Paperback)
978-1-4602-5509-4 (eBook)

1. Poetry, American

Distributed to the trade by The Ingram Book Company

I can remember every space I stood, every emotion I felt that led to every single poem in this book. They are meant to inspire change, to question and challenge the "self," to promote spiritual and emotional growth, to teach, but not hurt.

The moment has come for me to gather all of my stuff, then take up this pen and run; to dig deep into the past, reach for the future; before I lose the words –the ones that are whispered; and wake me up with a longing to dare, to dream, to be... Moments awaken, cannot be shaken. So I dare to dream, to write...

Mitzie Holstein

Dedicated to my mom and dad, Vincent and Rebertha, who knew that I was a poet since birth; to my husband, Richard, for giving me room to write; and to my sons, Sheldon and Joshua, for fanning the flames that have kept me going...

Activated

Merrily
Away
She wrote
Guided by voices
From an inner note

A Writer's Pen

Sometimes I become possessed
As I sit around and pen
The things on my mind
Or the happenings around me
It is not an obsession
But a possession of the soul
A yearning to exhale
To protest
To try to make things right
Deep inside
Is the yearning to fight
Not to run or take flight
So I wonder
I ponder
I think
I dream
Of what being me must mean
To someone who hates my guts
But who cannot keep me in a rut
That's when I take my pen
Deep in the pit of my mind I descend
And like a scavenger
I dig and search
Until on the tip of my tongue
Words perch
To be used

Not abused
When the opportune moment comes
From a place
That is safe
Not corrupt
Because I have been freed
From the barriers around
Never will my pen make a sound

Saturday

It's Saturday
Sabbath
Shabbat
And I just want to write
My best poems are written on Saturdays
I think better on Saturdays
I don't always have to be in a building
With people who feign love
To fellow men
On Saturdays
I can stay home and be by myself
With God
And me
My family
If I want on Saturdays
Or I can just be me
And be alone
To write
To think
"Perchance to dream"
On Saturdays

CREATIVE STREAMS

Movement

Movement is travel
Move
Move the head
Move the waist
Move the arms
Move the hands
Move the feet
Move the shoulders
The fingers
The hair
The toes
Just move
Move the body

CREATIVE STREAMS

Don't stop
Move until the sweat begins to drop
Just move
Work the body
Don't stop
Only then will the shape go pop!
Move for yourself
Not for anyone else
Move like your life depends on it
Just move
Get the body in groove
Just move!

I Am

I am the deep blue waters of the Caribbean sea
So don't you dare try to decipher me
When golden sunrays filter through my curtain
I am warm and strong
Strong enough to move you along
With just a little help from the wind
As she pushes against my body she's my friend
She tickles my soul as she makes big and small waves from my skin
And as my rival she cohorts with the rain to bring me pain
And by then I am so enraged I devour everything in sight
I roar against the rocks and I am dark and no longer blue
The sun and sky are no longer my friends
And those who live within me I do not defend
Soon I'll be calm again but do not trust
I'll suck you in like a whirlpool deep in my gut
This is me
It's who I am

Onward!

The principal says
Write us a poem for peace
I jump into action to please
Coworkers say publish your poems
One day I think
Not knowing how
Oprah says do what you love
Follow your passion
It resonated nicely
Then fell like a soft cushion
Until today
Today of all days
Came my "aha" moment
A day off from work
To catch myself
Then from the floodgates of my mind
It came
Like a dusty old trophy
Taken from off a shelf
I am a poet
That's what I am
Write! Write! Write!

Me

I come from a singing family
But I did not sing
One of two middle children
Who wanted to do her thing
Soon the time came for me to soar
I stood on stage and heard the applause from the floor
A poet! That's what I'll be
Thought about it for an eternity
Then I turned fourteen and my headmaster said
Poets don't make money
What would you like to do instead?
A nurse said I from out of the blue
Not daring to dream
Of being a writer or teacher too
Many years passed by
When at last!
I finally stood in front of a class
Motivating students
To write a difficult thing
Until I shifted gears to poetry
And watched their minds sing

CREATIVE STREAMS

I Sit And Write

I sit and write
Because it takes the blues away
Doing so keeps depression at bay
I sit and write because it makes me feel
My mind does not move like a ferris wheel
I sit and write because it's fun
Like daffodils swaying in the sun

I sit and write
I write and sit
Therefore my mind will never quit
To write the things
I feel
That's right
Bringing them to everyone's sight

I love to sit
And write a bit
Maybe one day the words will become a hit
Touching the heart of someone dear
Casting away all fears and tears

On Loving, etc...

Learning to Love

To watch young children play
To hear them speak
No malice
With sincerity
Usually very meek
And when at times they get angry
It all gets solved in a jiffy
Then they go back to play
Lots of smiles
Every day
Children have taught me how to love
Their actions
Not spiteful
Their love
Unconditional
They fight
They cry
Then get back
To holding hands
No grudges held
That's the love
Teaching children has taught me

Bleach Not Thy Skin

Bleach not thy skin
For it does not make you pure within
But work to retain a heart
Pure and true
A heart filled with love
One that makes your life anew
Bleach not thy skin for goodness sake
It was not God's design
Not what He tried to make
Instead, work from the inside out
Let God design the route
Live earnestly
Live peacefully
Follow His will
Say Peace! Be still!
Guard the heart
Guard the mind

Remember that you
Are one of a kind
God made you. He made me too
Let Him change you from within
No outside bleaching
He is far reaching
You are beautiful the way you are

Fairer than the morning star
So no bleaching please
I beg of you
Your self-concept must be guided
By you and only you
Love yourself
For who you are
Only self-love will carry you far

Marriage Rules

One day you meet
And sparks fly
You hold hands
Kiss
Make love
You know that he's the one for you
Soon you get married
Settle down
You lose the romance
You start to fight
Where has the love gone?
True love endures
Is forgiving
Willing to say sorry
So if you think you have found it
Cherish it
Make it happen
Fix the negatives
Embellish the positives
Add a bit of trust
Do not subject your relationship to the past
Continue to learn
To grow
Make up
Hold hands

Pray for guidance
Make God the center
Lessen the stress
Do not go fifty-fifty
100% is what you need
All of you
Only then will you be complete
Then count your blessings
Lessen the complaints
Admit that you are not perfect
And love each other
Over and over and over again

Home

Is your home
A place where you raise your children?
Invite family in
Friends to chat
Stay a while
But then
Must go
Is a home a place for sacrifice
Fulfillment
Dreams achieved
Or is it a place
Where people come and go
Become unattached
Displaced
Conspirators
A rental space
For things not your own
I dream of a home
Where friends come and go
Stay a while to chat

Then must go
I dream of a home
Where families can
Be invited in – very briefly

And then move on
I dream of a home
That gives life to my children
A place for them to just be
And then move off into life with mirth
Resounding
Independence abounding
To return
To recapture
The joys of youth
The wisdom of old age
A home
Where lives collide
On a stage
Predetermined by time

There are Times

There are times when
You try to see the bigger picture
Even though you are just a small speck
But there are times
When things don't add up
And you just want to do
To say something
But you keep it
Bottled up deep inside
Sometimes you let it out in groans
A whisper
A prayer
Sometimes you say what the...!
Soon enough
You begin to realize
That it's not worth it
To worry so much
To care too deeply
To censor oneself
In the end it often works out
The player gets played

The foolish turn wise
Sometimes too late
We just need to
Let it all hang out
And one day
One day
Motives are revealed
Truth stands
Hope returns
And love will continue to abound
Above all else

About My Parents

Between my mom and dad
I am the darkest child
My youngest sister was called
Red Devil – out of love
By an aunt who spoiled her
She was tomboyish, red
Some called me Black Monkey
But we were kids
I got over those minute skids
Because of my parents
Their unconditional love
Not one put down
In them was found
They helped to build my self-esteem
Got some licks
Had to scream
But they loved me
The best they could
Provided
Guided
Never derided
Today I stand proud
And can shout out very loud
Mom! Dad!

I am who I am because of
you
So if I seem over confident
It's my swag
Of all the ills that life has
yielded
LOVE
Conquered all
It used my
Jamaican parents

CREATIVE STREAMS

A Bit of Fantasy?

Man's Torment

When love becomes hate
It spoils the essence of life itself
When peace becomes war
It tears up and breaks down
The home
The church
The school
The community and the country
And in the end
The whole world will break out
In a sweat
A sweat that will spoil
Human
Food and animal flesh
Everything will rot
Break down
And fester
The children of men will cry from
hunger
There will be death and strife
Among every living thing
Even the dead will groan in their graves
The ancestors long gone
Will rise up

Their voices will echo
And be heard over all others
They will cry mostly for the children
Who are dying, have died

And continue to die
That is because man has gone mad
Crazier than the wild dogs that roam the
forest
At night looking for blood
And in the end
The souls of the dead will go back to
their graves
And there shall be no rest for them
Because man has not changed his ways
They will moan silently
They will not rest
Until man has changed his ways

CREATIVE STREAMS

Dreaming in the Wind

One day in spring
I met a guy
And oh how our hearts melted
Love bloomed and blossomed
Our hearts became one
We were inseparable
The summer came
We went on strolls
Hearts and hands intertwined
We laughed out loud
As children would
We had our heart's desire
The fall wind blew
And somehow I knew
Our lives began to change
The hugs grew less
My heart sunk low
I was a living mess
Suddenly it was winter
I needed warmth
But when I turned
He was not there
His heart was stone
His eyes were cold
I must have been dreaming in the wind
Now dreaming in the wind

Is all I do
Dreaming in the wind
When I think of you
Dreaming in the wind
Can set your heart afire
Dreaming in the wind
Will stifle your desire

CREATIVE STREAMS

Dreams

There was a time
When I was young
And thought of lovely things
Then I grew up and realized
That all I had were dreams
Dreams come from the heart
They'll always stay with you
Dreams all come from the heart
Let them not depart from you
One day I sat
Just by the pond
To watch fish dip and dive
My mind was ablaze
And spun in a haze
My dreams became alive
Dreams
They never leave you
Dreams
They never fail
Take time to dream big
Your dreams will amaze and inspire you
Just stay within your dreams

Dare to Dream

Dare to dream
Dream for those who fail to
Dream the impossible
And aspire towards the unthinkable
Dare to dream
Dreams open the eyes to a world of possibilities
Never cease to dream
Dreams incite hope
Hope for aspirations unheard of
Hope that all dreams will come true
Dare to dream
Dreams are what we are made of
Life's dreams promise hope for the future
So keep dreaming
Dare to dream

My Fantasy

You look at me with dark brown eyes
Eyes that say
I've known you all my life
I look at you and your deep
Sunken eyes
Look almost like mine
Every time I see you
You never keep conversation
Yet you say – Hi, how are you?
I must have met you before
In another life
Maybe
I still hope to see you tomorrow
The next day and the day after that
You make my days always enjoyable
Suddenly you're no longer there
I search for you
In the valleys of my mind
You are etched in the Kodak part of my
memories
You!
With your beautiful dark skin
And short curly hair
Your height does not matter to me
If only I could see you
I would tell you how much I feel

This forbidden love
Can't be for real
I am dumbstruck now that you've
appeared
Your big beautiful smile is thrilling me to
my very bones
I am very happy and I hope
That you'll not take
My quietness as an insult
I want to jump, cry, run
Yet, I only smile
'Cause with you
There's no space
No time!

To My Poet Friend

The day my teacher told me that poetry was a hobby
I allowed it to dissipate from my mind
Eighteen years later I met you and you changed everything
You
Black star apple from my father's tree
Like its juice
Your teeth sparkle white
Your words as sweet as the core
You!
Dark prince of Africa
I am caught up in your spell
What kind of web have you woven?
Now there is fire in my soul
Fire for you
Fire that burns my fingers
As they pause on this white sheet of paper
I am now your poetess for life
Is there such a word
Please tell me
For I will not rest

Until you have taken all the words from my heart and made them yours
Until you have surrendered the core of your being to me
So that I can taste you
Like the star apple
I fear that you will not submit
Unless you are shaken or picked
I have chosen you
My inspiration
My poet friend

CREATIVE STREAMS

Suicide

I thought of suicide
So I decided to check myself in
Totally against my morals
One of the greatest sins

I thought of suicide
To end life as it is
Hopelessly alone
Thoughts moving about like a drone

Ideas lurking
Mind becomes stagnant
Dark thoughts sleeping
My only tenants

Thinking of suicide
Bad state of affairs
Feeling deep inside that no one cares

Thought of suicide
And how it would end
No more in glory
Would my spirit ascend
So I checked myself in to the Man above
And he whispered softly
I'll send you my heavenly dove

Reality

To Eryka Love

Dare to be daring
Always caring
Teacher, leader
A queen when you meet her
Regal
Classy
Works from the heart
Always stands tall
Even when things
Seem to want
To fall apart
Outspoken, unbroken, resolute
You are amazing queen
Beauty reflected
Your poise your style
Your YOU
Stand steadfast
Though the tides may swirl
Stand steadfast
Give a queenly twirl

You are you
I am me
But I accept you as Queen Bee
Run from greatness you shall not
God has planted you in that spot
Your beauty lies at the core
Heaven will provide so much more
Ah! To think an open door
So here's to you my sister queen
You deserve all this and more
Just not yet seen

Know Your Crowd

Not everyone who laughs and talks with you
Is for you
Know your crowd
They might even share some secrets
But they are still not for you
Know your crowd
They may go to church with you
That does not make them a part of you
Understand this...
They may eat with you too
But didn't Judas eat with Jesus?
Know your crowd
For it's the hard times that shape the size
Of your crowd
The ones who pray for you
The ones who call when they can't show up
To hear you or give a word of cheer
The ones who check in just to let you know
That they are there
Recognize!
Your crowd might be bigger
Or smaller than you may think
Know your circle
Know your crowd

A Father Is

A father is someone who is always strong
He makes you feel better when everything has gone wrong
He'll make you laugh he'll make you cry
He wants you to marry the right kind of guy
A father will take you to watch the cricket match down the street
He'll carry you on his shoulder to the next soccer meet
He'll buy you a bellyful on a hot summer's day
He'll bring KFC at night if Mom says it's ok
A father is loveable he can be lots of fun
But don't take him for granted or soon all the fun will be done
He'll lay down the rules he will not let you act the fool
He is the ultimate in cool
A happy Father's Day to dads young and old
You're worth all of life's treasures much more than gold
If anyone should ask what makes you unique
Tell them that God gave you a special technique
To love your children and adore
The good and bad that come to the fore

Random

We always meet as strangers
Then friendships form
Simplistic
Complicated
Engaging
Refreshing
Exhausting
We cherish
We nourish
We soothe
We heal
We impede
We crush
We bemoan
We shatter
All at random

America the Great (originally America Post 9/11)

Land of freedom
Land of war
Land of peace
There you are
America
Land of Spirit
Truth and grace
Land that will never quit the race
May you fight until you're done
Because the battle
Has not yet been won
America
Land of the beautiful
Land of the free
Bring the enemy to his knee
May his conscience sear his soul
Till the bell of victory tolls

America!
This is America
Land of the brave
Though you hurt us
Our banners continue to wave
High above the skies
Our spirits soar
As we replace future's door
America!

For the Victims of 9/11

Your families watched as you left for work
Were you angry?
Did you even say goodbye?
How could you?
Who did not know
That you were about to die
I did not know you
But I felt it when I heard
The devastating news
My knees became weak
But I had to remain strong
For the students
Who depended on me to lead
Firemen
Policemen
Peace officers
Office workers and civilians
This is all for you
Yet at the time when we seem all together
The division breaks my heart asunder
Funds for family of the firemen, policemen too
Just call it the Victim's Fund
Add the money together
Divide it amongst them all
They were all victims
Regardless of their status before death

What of the mother
Who lost her only son?
What about the widow
Whose husband's salary was her only income?
He could be a fireman, a civilian
A policeman too
Still he deserves the equality
That will cause hope to renew
For the families
The city and the country
We have lost
We have mourned
Still mourn
But we must move on
Equity in life and death
Will mean that a victory
Has been won

Through It All – Mimicking Dr. Maya Angelou

You may tear me down like old wallpa-
per
You might slaughter my name
That will not matter
Because I'll always remain the same
You can pretend that you like me
When deep down it's a sham
Rest assured that I don't give a damn
You live in misery all day long
And each time it's the same old song
Just take the time to uncover your face
Haven't you gotten older than the
Rest of the human race
Then you marvel because I walk with a
beat
You say, Girl you look so
Young and sweet
But your flattery doesn't work
That's because deep down
I know that you're a jerk
I continue to live my life
As I've always done
Not trying to keep up with the Joneses
Just having my kind of fun
I smile at my enemies
If I perceive them to be

I laugh with my friends
If they choose to laugh with me
What's the secret? You may ask
Isn't it a daunting task?
Certainly not!
My response will be
That's because I have chosen to be me
I laugh plenty
I laugh loud
My life is not surrounded by one big
cloud
I can see the good in the bad
I can see the forest from the trees
That's because I am
The eternal optimist
And there are no bad thoughts
For anyone on MY WISH LIST

Friendship

I see a side of you that I see in me
Pretty, cheery personality
Bright shiny white smile that makes my day
When we go out together
Girl power rules sista!
I still see you moving your feet
To the beat of the salsa music
I watch you with envy and pride
As I try to learn the steps
I'm nervous
But your encouragement drives me on
And I owe my newfound knowledge
Of that dance to you
That's why I feel it when you're sad
You, who are always jolly
You, the one yellow flower
In a garden full of weeds
You are rare
As few of my best friends are
You stand unique because you are you
Among the weeds you stand
Pretty yellow flower

CREATIVE STREAMS

Message for the Jilted Bride

Don't be so naïve woman
You are only fooling yourself
Maybe he did you a favor
At least there was no one else
Or was there?
Were you too pushy
Did he feel smothered
Take a look at yourself woman
You will be less bothered
You want to know why he did it
But indeed you know
Time for deep introspection woman
You are reaping what you have sown
Some say love is blind
That's what we think
Maybe he didn't want to mess up
A good thing
I know what it's like when a woman's in love
And when he's great
We think he's sent from above
We want to hold him close
And keep him to ourselves
When suddenly he realizes
That he's losing himself
Why don't you marry?
Everyone else says

Mom, Dad
Other family and friends
So you decide to do the right thing
That's for sure
Suddenly he's not certain
Anymore
But you want to marry him
And he seems to want it too
Only,
He doesn't want it as badly as you

Poor jilted bride
Now you are all alone
You seek the spotlight
And you moan and groan
You loved him
He loved you
You both loved each other
Maybe marriage was meant for another
Not him!
He felt smothered and he let you go
Thank God it happened so

Plight of a Caregiver

She watches me with deeply sunken eyes
Eyes old from misery
Pain
Shame
Strong
Weak
Tired eyes
Trying to penetrate my existence
Eyes that once had happiness too
Years of experience
Still lingers
Behind those sockets
Deep into the walls of her brain
Out of her mouth
Come minute words of wisdom
Strength and courage
Out of that mouth
Come nonsensical sentences
I pretend to comprehend
And sometimes I do
'Cause if I don't who else will?
Her loved ones will not understand
And at times do not care
They expect everything from me
The one whom she holds dear

But why does she?
She who tries to spit at me

She, who has thrown water on me
Let us blame it on the brain
That tells her when to be nice
It's only Alzheimer's
That's her plight

CREATIVE STREAMS

A Recruit's Poem

Be my rock
Be my soldier
Be my guide during road marches
Early in the morning
When it's cold and rainy
When water runs off my body
And my heavy basic dress uniform
Itches my skin
And as the distance gets longer
And the heavy dirt road
Connives to pull me forward
Into its tracks of slush and mud
Give me words of encouragement
My boots might be heavy
But I will keep moving forward
Do not hold my hand
But be there for me if I do fall
Do not yell and scream
For I shall not hear you
And when the sun shows its yellow face
And the final drops of rain have gone

I will be closer to the end of one road
march yet again
My body will be cold and between my
legs chaffed
But there will be no respect lost for you
My drill sergeant

Religiosity

We sit numb in our seats
Silenced by the voices
Of those who claim
To speak for God
And we say nothing!
We accept mediocrity
Wear it as a cloak
We can no longer discern
We listen as children
Participate in the sac-religious
And we say nothing
We have become like sheep
Led astray by wolves
Dressed as sheep
We can hear
We can see
But we say nothing
They thump the Bible's pages
They seem to speak the truth
But we have forgotten
Not everyone that says, "Lord, Lord"
Will enter the Master's heaven
Still we say nothing
God needs authentic
Organic praise
He needs our hearts

We need to open our eyes
Not everyone is led by the spirit
But Satan has so many of us under lock-
down
We say that we are free
Yet we are not liberated
We say that we are strong
But where is our strength
We do not love
We remain unforgiving
Our desire has shifted to money – not
God
We love ourselves
We take pride in our possessions
We do not give the needy the attention
They deserve
Our soup kitchens are only pacifiers
That cover a deeper problem
And we continue to remain silent
I am afraid for myself
Afraid but brave enough
To realize that the God in me
Is not about my degrees
He is the same all knowing
Who knows and accepts me
I laud and adore His name

Because He has been good to me
He is merciful and forgiving
He does not want us to play CHURCH
Neither does He want us to sit in the pews
And accept all of the prosperity ideas
Being spewed from the mouths
Of sinful people like ourselves
We can only give Him our all
That's the single seed that we can sow
So no longer will I remain silent
I will reject the past patterns
And conditions
That have so far condemned and enslaved me
I will walk freely in the liberty
Where Christ has made me free
For He has broken the chains of slavery
I am liberated
Therefore
I will not remain silent

CREATIVE STREAMS

In Motion-At The Airport

Line up!
People are driven
Away they go
Piling away
Filing away
Flying away
To places
Spaces filled
Abandoned
To be explored
And adored
In single files they pass
Ready to mingle for the right cause
They stop
They eat
Then off again
To find a gate that leads them there
Not knowing when or if
They'll ever be seen again
They walk in lines
Or side-to-side
Colors bloom cheerfully on their bodies
Some slim
Some fat
Some this
Some that

In motion
They ebb
They flow
Like the tide
Swinging high and low
In motion
Taking only their portion
People on track to destinations unknown
Yet they continue to be in motion
Man, woman, boy, girl
Eyes filled with wonder
Like a pearl
Still going
Still moving
Airplanes sounding
Spaces abounding
As up they go
In motion!

Dedicated to You, Robin Williams- Suicide

Nobody knew of the pain
The thing that drove you insane
Trying to stay true to the self
While working to please everyone else

No one understood
And you could not explain
That the life you lived
Felt like it was in vain

You used laughter as a cover
From the hurts
The pains
The loneliness you felt
Deep within the pit of you it dwelt

Eating you up slowly
Deep inside
Became your landlord
Took over your pride
And ended in suicide

What is a Friend?

Friends come
Friends go
They are with you during highs
They stay with you during lows
And even if the friendship ends
Never too low will they descend

They will stay true
To the idea of what once was
Will sometimes grieve
That there might have been no reprieve

Secrets they will never tell
Knowing that you have been privy
To theirs as well
And if they have nothing good to say
Will aim to keep naysayers at bay

And when exes come around
Wanting to take a final pound
Such will be sent away
A great friend will not sway
Would never pound your name in the
dust
Even after your friendship
Has developed some rust

Never jealous of friendship that's new
Knowing that great friends are just a few
A friend will always be a friend
Even if the friendship ends

Rebellion

Fear

We live in an era of fear
Fear to love
Fear to give
Fear to move
Fear to live
We allow ourselves to be controlled
By others
We fear about how they view us
We fear what they might do to us
We live in fear of tyranny
From those who are set to rule over us
So we become numb
Dumb
We refuse to speak
"Cat's got our tongues"
We are crippled
Paralyzed by fear
Not wanting to lose
What we hold as dear
But why fear man
When God has the master plan
Live life to the fullest
Don't you fret
Fear God almighty
He's not through with you yet
He rules the heavens

And the earth
Live as if He is your maker
For He's the creator
Lose the fear
Hold Him near
Man's not God
Have no fear

CREATIVE STREAMS

I Speak My Mind

Every now and then
I silence my mouth
I silence myself
But every now and then
A fire sparks
And I speak up
I speak up for those who fear to speak
I speak up for those whose voices are
Smothered by tyranny
I speak my mind
For the little child who hears when the
word
"Animal" is used to describe him or her
But sometimes I remain silent
I cannot fight every fight
Yet I am "my brother's keeper"
So in a while
I will erupt in a stream of heat
Madness
When folly reigns and good sense is lost
When blame takes over
And good intent is thrust aside
I open my mouth
I speak my mind
And when words fail
It can be seen in my eyes

They become intense
In my walk
It says
I don't give a ... about you!
'Cause you do not care about me
Or my good intentions
Or our children
By then I do not care what you say
I can see it in your walk
Your look
Hear it from your lips – at times
For now I have quieted
But the soul is awake
Because it is saddened by the bull...
The fakery, the pretense
It is discomfited
So as long as I live
I will forever speak my mind
Even eons after you
Have cut out my tongue

I Stand

I stand
Adrift in thought
Wondering
How did it get to this?
Amazed
That one human being
Could have worked on you
And drenched your self-esteem

In bitterness
Streaming like blood
From the mouth of a serpent
Hating on you
Sabotaging your spirit
Robbing you of your soul

But you continued to love
In spite of
You dared to hope
To dream
To wish
To long
To become
Holding on
To promises broken
Words spoken
Redeeming nothing

But you held on
Dreaming
Wishing
Hoping for change

But those words still linger
In your head
Making you feel lifeless and dead
Like dirt
Twisted inside
With the mind of a child

You left love
It found you back
And it bit you hard like a viper
Those words
Poured out on you
Belittling your existence
Drenching you with madness
As you steep inside
Ready to explode
Ready to revolt
And when you ask
Why do you act this way?
To frighten you a bit
Love would say

Then you begin to question love
And realized
That he was just a copycat
A fake
A user, an abuser

So you took heart
Got brave and ran
Ran as fast as you could
All your prayers answered
And you knew
Fake is what sat
Where love once stood

Memories

Where Were You? (A Dedication to Michael Jackson)

Were you on the street
In a crowd or by yourself in a room
Did you cry for yourself
For him
For who he was
Or for whom you thought he'd become
Where were you on the day he died
How did you feel
Were you simply heartbroken
Did you rejoice
Or were you too overwhelmed to react
And on July 7, 2009 where were you
In a crowd
At the Staples Center
Or did you just sit in your room and cry?

For Cousin Rohan – Unbelievable

I spoke to you on Friday
And you were gone on Monday
Unbelievable!
Unbelievable that your parents no longer have a first-born
Your brothers
An older brother
Your children
No father
Unbelievable!
We all mourn your passing
Not knowing of your sufferings
So easygoing you were
So respectful too
That's why it's unbelievable
It's all unbelievable because of who you were
People couldn't help loving you
Cannot stop missing you
But you're gone
Now isn't that unbelievable?
So many precious moments shared

Talking
Laughing
Gonna come to my birthday party?
A wha yuh a sey Mitzie?
Mummy, yuh cook?
And so many plans
Then there's "Prini" Princess
The love of your life
No wonder
We keep wondering
Why it's so unbelievable

Mind's Confusion

My mind is perturbed
Just like the murky waters that line Jamaican trenches
After a heavy downpour of rain
Like the water that gushes down the gully
And gets sucked in by the sinkhole that lies at the bottom
Waiting with wide, open mouth
Waiting to gobble it up
With one big, mighty sup
Water that contains pieces of human waste
That boys have secretly passed out
On stones close by the pond
Dead leaves
Banana trees
Old tin cans rooted up from where long buried
Like memories from childhood
A childhood that was good and bad
That's my brain
That's my mind
But when the rains have stopped
And the rushing waters have subsided
The sun will come out and make everything almost brand new
Bad memories will have gone
Or would have sunken somewhere far beyond
Then will I be free to be me
And my mind shall not be perturbed

I Took A Ride

Took a ride around the island
Not all-just part
Went to the South Coast
With its hills and vales
The sun streaming into the car
Hot wind fanning my face
We became one
In love
Still in love with Jamaica
Got to the plains
Where Little Ochi stood
Backed by the waves and Dark sand
dunes
Placed an order
Waited while fish cooked
Sat in solace
I had reached heaven
The wind blew
I felt alive
I moaned
Sighed
Could have cried
But there was no need
My heart did not bleed
I was home and in love with Jamaica

I watched children play
As the cool wind caressed and soothed
my soul
So in love
In love with Jamaica

The food came
I ate
Licked my lips
Steamed fish with okra and bami, crack-
ers, festival
I moaned
I sighed
Could have cried
But there was no need
My heart did not bleed
I had a need
Filled it indeed
Of love for Jamaica

Every Now and Then

Every now and then
I like to take my pen
And travel deep inside my mind
To search as if it were a den
Locked up for years
Ready to loosen
Those animals that conquer my fears

Every now and then
I like to take up my pen
And travel to distance space
To find memories that no one can erase
And on paper they explode
Steamy and hot without any abode
The memories that make me laugh and sway
Ones that make me breathe
Alert and alive each day

So every now and then
I like to take my pen
And make a trip in that mind of mine
To conquer
To release
To face the past
Embrace the future at last
It all happens
Every now and then

Take Me Away

Take me away to Jamaica
Where the sights and sounds
Tingle the senses
Where the pungent scent of smoke
From the fireside
Brings back memories of childhood

Take me away to Jamaica
Where the hills stand resolute
And the plains remain still
Yet alive
Alive with the sound of waves
Crashing against shorelines
Where the voices of children linger
Where the sun beams in its majesty
And skins turn red, deep bronze or dark

Take me away to Jamaica
Where streams run into rivers
Where springs supply women, men folk
and children
With mineral water rare
And the water
Sweet and cool to the taste
While bubbles saunter to the top
Like fish rushing to find food above

Take me away to Jamaica
Where mosquitoes sing and bite
A song so annoyingly sweet
And a hit that is planned
Where hand and insect will surely meet

Take me away to Jamaica
Where the thought of food
Becomes a conquest
A longing to taste only the best
Whether steamed, jerked, roasted or
fried
Fish, meat and things
One of a kind

Take me away to Jamaica
Where summer never ends
A simple slice of heaven
No need to play Lucky Seven

Take me away to Jamaica
Where it's forever grand
Where people will always strive
To lend each other a helping hand

Take me away to Jamaica
Give me my bush tea

To make the body ready
Make all the illness flee

Take me away to Jamaica
Land of the rising sun
Where everyone gets rowdy
Until the fun gets done

Take me away to Jamaica
Land of wood and water
Where Dunns River Falls
Beckons and calls
And memories stand up tall

Take me away to Jamaica
A place I long to see
A yearly trek
With many on deck
Jamaica the place to be

History in Motion

History in Motion

Crowds a moving
People a grooving
Multitudes mixing
Bodies fixing
Colors black red blue and white
Juxtaposed!
Oh what a terrific sight!
People of all different hues
Cheeks cold and turning blue
With feet walking steadfastly
Forwarding into history
Oh how I marvel at this mystery!
Blending with the surroundings
In an ocean's swell of pride
Longing for peace and love to abide
Bodies in motion
With the energy of a potion
Moving along without any commotion
Streaming!
Faces gleaming
Simply flowing
Just going and going
Inaugural Park
Moving in-between light and dark
Faces going places
The intermingling of the races

Jamming into crowded spaces
As they sing Obama's praises
Not red states,
Or blue states
Neither white
Nor black
Just simply people
Moving to one destination
With history as our teacher
America
Once again
Leader of the pack

A Star is Born

Born from a broken home
Born to be free
Son of a single mother
Dad chose to flee
A star you are
And a star you'll be
Aspiring to take us all
Far into the next century

President Obama
Son of this soil
Sleeves rolled up
Never afraid to toil
You are American
You are one of us
We are all travelling
On the same bus
Even though the economy is failing
And the bus dangles near the railing
Hope is in sight
If we follow
The star's light
A star he is
A star he'll be
The next president
Of our country

Full Speed Ahead

Full speed ahead my child
God is right by your side

Full speed ahead my child
Hate will not come close to
Where love abides

Full speed ahead my child
No turning back
You've got nothing to hide
And He is on your side

Full speed ahead my son
You've changed the course of history
Something never thought could be done

Go forth in peace my child
Let not pride in your heart abide
Stand firm in your beliefs
As others watch in disbelief

Now full speed ahead my child
Do your job with pride
Thus saith the Lord!
For he has spoken
And his words can never be broken

As you go full speed ahead
Tarry for the living and not for the dead
Don't forget to keep the Lord in view
No matter what valley you
might be travelling through

Go forth in peace my child
Full speed ahead
You are Barack Obama
Born to lead
No longer will you be judged
by your color or creed

So full speed ahead
Never look back
God is taking you on a journey
He has got your back!

CREATIVE STREAMS

Unbelievable

When you were born the stars in the
galaxy twinkled and smiled with glee
Angels sang because you were going to
be one special man
Unbelievable!

Unbelievable that you were born to
aspire towards the unthinkable
No earthly force could stop you because
when the angels sang
They already knew that you were going
to do things insurmountable
That's why you're unbelievable

And the birds chirped and whispered
songs of hope on the day of your birth
The bees pollinated each flower being
fully aware of the change that was yet to
come
And the butterflies intermingled and
layed eggs that began a new
species spelled HOPE
The sun shone
And its radiance was reflected on your
face
The moon stood huge and
still at night and smiled

There was change in the air
With great hope and without any
thought of despair
You were THE ONE
Who was sent to fulfill the master's plan
Teaching us all to live as one
As we continue our journey in this land

President Obama chosen by God
Proclaiming hope for the future in this
our native land
Calling for change that was never heard
before
It stuck to the heart of people hoping for
an opening to
Future's door
Oh how sweet it has become to be a
present witness to the unbelievable

Never in a lifetime would this happen we
all said
But no one knew of the plans that lay
ahead
The plan that was set by One from on
high
Who lives much further
than the clear blue sky

So here's the message that He has given me to give to you
Something on which to ponder when you are feeling blue:
Now is not the time to falter my child
Now is not the time to wane
You have achieved the impossible
Now full speed ahead to make others realize the unbelievable

Keep that smile on your face
You're supported by God's grace
May His goodness shine on you
No matter what tides or storms you'll have to swim through
As you continue to forge ahead
Destined to do what many continue to think was impossible, unthinkable and still
UNBELIEVABLE!

Random Thoughts

When the Wind Blows

When the wind blows
Leaves rustle
And trees bend
Plants sway
Time passes us by
When the wind blows

When

We stay locked
In our corners
Wanting to escape
Longing to be free
Or be freed by something
Or someone
But when?

Through My Window

I feel a great degree of peace engulf me
Whenever I look through my window
The window
Through it I am beginning to find inner peace
I need nothing else

The Storm

Inside I stand
Outside I look
Searching for the path
That nature took
The wind blows hard
The branches bend
In reverence to nature's fury
Raindrops falling swiftly
Manipulated by the wind's intensity
No longer like tears
But like falling spaghetti

Nature

Green as the grass
Green as the trees
Flowers abuzz
With busy bees
Just like spring
When from the earth
Has sprung
New life in nature has just begun
With a flower
Here and there
Bringing thankfulness and cheer

Summer Musings

Looking through my window
Feeling the wind on my face
Watching cars, people and buses go by
Ah! The spirit of the human race
For a while
Troubles disappear
No talk of the rent due
Do I want to hear
Just let me sit or lay
On my bed
And watch cars
People
And buses
As they go by

My Child

You look up at me with bright shiny eyes
And I am love struck
I wanted you from the beginning
You whom I've dreamt about all my life
And in my dreams
There you were
Smiling up at me
Looking just like my brother
I've felt pain for you
Deep in my loins
When you hurt I hurt too
Do not cry my love
Act like a member of your species
Cry only when necessary
You are your mother's child
You will never ever be abandoned by her
Here's what I give to you son
Love unconditional
I am
Your mother

Man

You are the imperfect
Perfection of God's creation
You do the things I like
You talk to me
You are very affectionate
You'll tell me if I'm wrong
Whenever I become despondent and weak
You teach me the art
Of forbearance and strength
Still you are
A total contradiction
You continue to do the things I hate
You're conniving and slippery
I fail to understand how one man
Can be so complicated
Yet so grand
Perhaps I should have taken more time to think
Before I made you
An additional part
Of my destiny

Musings

Here we are again
Same old house
Same old job
It's an everyday thing
Now it's so routine
I can't even tell the difference
This is not me I say
So why make the change
I'm afraid
Afraid that I won't be accepted
Afraid that my skills won't match up
Afraid
That the next person
Might be better than me

Contradiction (Originally, Reasons)

I do not feel
The pain that everybody feels
I do not care to listen to them either
I do not care about helping them
To overcome their hurts
Because in them
My hurts
My pains
My fears
Are reproduced
Still, only then can I deal with them
So when I help others
I wind up helping myself

CREATIVE STREAMS

Contradictions

I am certain that there is indeed a God
A God who bears no ill will towards us
Yet we will often use any opportunity
To break each other down
Instead of
Building each other up
When people wrong us
We become discouraged
Yet there are those who will use any
Opportunity as a stepping-stone
To score a point
To not be the loser
And when the oppressed
Becomes the oppressor
Out goes sanity
In flies insanity
I know that we must do to others
What we expect of ourselves
Love holds no grudges
Does not incite hate
Does not tempt
Does not participate in blackmail
Or extortion
There is nothing uglier
Than seeing a person on a vendetta
Being bitter or vindictive

I loathe mischief
I abhor mischief-makers
I fight my fights
Might even fight your fights too
But in my heart
I know mischief whenever I see it
"God does not like ugly" as some would say
When he gives us a chance to escape a situation
We must use it for the greater good
We must NOT
See it as an opportunity to get even
To make others PAY
Then we would have lost sight of
His goodness
What He truly is all about
For "God is love"
And love is of God
So let's work to cheer someone today
Especially one
Who seems unlovable

Gold Standard-Mom Inspired

Ever wonder why people look at you?
Judge you?
Criticize you?
That's because you are the standard
The gold standard
You have set the bar high
Too high for some to reach

Some will love you
Some will hate you
Some will mock, mimic or scourge you
Because you are gold
Tried in the fire
Smelted
Burnished
Proven
Now it's your turn to shine

Gold standard speaks volumes
It says you have made it
You have overcome a lot
A trendsetter it's not
That comes and goes like the wind
Or the tide
It ebbs and flows

Gold is authentic
Not fake
Expensive
Not corrosive
Proven over time
Not plated but real

Are you gold standard?
Have you set the pace for members of
your family
And race?
Gold standard takes courage
Boldness
Truth
Being true to who you are
Leaving hate and anger afar
Gold standard finds favor
Is not corrupt
Is blessed by others
Pass on blessings to all
Picks you up whenever you fall
That's the gold standard
Are you?

Dark Thoughts

Seconds
Minutes
Hours
Days
Weeks
Months
Years
Suicide
Killing oneself
Seemingly happy
Dying inside from guilt
Shame
Being stressed out
Now it ends
In suicide

Reached the lowest of the lows
In your life
Then comes the moment
Fleeting, passing
You take a chance

You jump
Never to return
Dead, gone, forgotten

As your parents seethe
Try to heal
The disappointment of you
Being you
What you became
What you have done to them
More shame
More guilt
No surrender

Because you quickly wanted to meet
your maker
So you took life by surprise
And it ended in SUICIDE

Acknowledgements

I would like to acknowledge the effort that my elementary teachers at Wait-A-Bit All-Age School played in fostering my love of the spoken word. To my friends, Cedra Lewis-Baird and Coleen Gaynor, other dear friends as well as colleagues at Public School 276, thanks for believing in me.

Last, but certainly not least, homage must be paid to Dr. Maya Angelou, a true poet and "friend in my head," as well as my siblings and other family members who have remained a steady stream of motivation to me.

Above all else, I thank the Eternal Muse for bestowing me with this gift.

CPSIA information can be obtained at www.ICGtesting.com
Printed in the USA
BVIW12n0006110215
386783BV00006B/17